THE HIDDEN WORLD

The Story
of Microscopic Life

PAUL VILLIARD

with photographs
by the author

FOUR WINDS PRESS   NEW YORK

Other books by Paul Villiard

Collecting Stamps

Exotic Fish as Pets

Insects as Pets

Reptiles as Pets

Wild Mammals as Pets

Through the Seasons with a Camera

Moths and How to Rear Them

A First Book of Jewelrymaking

A First Book of Ceramics

A First Book of Leatherworking

A Manual of Veneering

Handy Man's Plumbing and Heating Guide

Growing Pains

The Practical Candymaking Cookbook

Shells—Homes in the Sea

LIBRARY OF CONGRESS CATALOGING IN PUBLICATION DATA
Villiard, Paul.
    The hidden world.
    SUMMARY: A guide to exploring the microscopic world
of plants and animals, including suggestions for photographing specimens and examining microscopic causes of air and
water pollution.
    1. Miscroscope and microscopy—Juvenile literature.
[1. Microscope and microscopy]   I.   Title.
QH278.V54   576   74–22153
              ISBN 0–590–07307–9

Published by Four Winds Press
A Division of Scholastic Magazines, Inc., New York, N.Y.
Copyright © 1975 by Gertrude Villiard
All Rights Reserved
Printed in the United States of America
Library of Congress Catalog Card Number: 74–22153
1   2   3   4   5   79   78   77   76   75

for
Gertrude

The world is so full of a number of things,
I'm sure we should all be as happy as kings.

ROBERT LOUIS STEVENSON
A Child's Garden Of Verses

Acknowledgments

THE AUTHOR WOULD LIKE TO EXTEND THANKS TO THE BAUSCH AND Lomb Optical Company of Rochester, New York, for its help in supplying the student microscopes used in the preparation of this book.

Mr. David Jones, Science Department, Saugerties Senior High School, Saugerties, New York, was of invaluable help with information, material, and loan of apparatus for the photographing of specimens.

Mr. William Robinson, of the Science Department of the Saugerties Junior High School, Saugerties, New York, also supplied material and information for the text.

My special thanks goes to Honeywell Photographic of Denver, Colorado, for supplying the Honeywell Pentax H3V camera and microscope adapter with which the majority of the photographs were taken.

In preparing this book I was fortunate to have the cooperation of Ward's Natural Science Establishment, in Rochester, New York, and of Dr. Gustav Garay, at the biological laboratory at Ward's, and I would like to extend by sincere thanks to them for their help with material and information in this work.

Contents

1

Exploring the Microscopic World

IF SOMEONE ASKED YOU TO NAME A PLANT, YOU WOULD probably first think of a flower, like a geranium or pansy, or a tree. There are 250,000 different species, or kinds, of plants living on earth. Almost half of the known plants are so small your eyes cannot see them.

The word *animal* probably brings to mind a dog or cat or any other animal you are used to seeing. Animals are either vertebrate, meaning they have a backbone, or invertebrate, meaning they do not have a backbone. Scientists know of about 55,000 species of vertebrate animals, and all are large enough to be seen with just your eyes. A dog is a vertebrate animal. Humans are vertebrate animals.

Most invertebrates are small animals. There are nearly one million known species of invertebrates, and scientists believe that there are many times that number not yet dis-

covered. Worms and insects are examples of invertebrates large enough to be seen.

The plants and invertebrate animals discussed in this book are but a few of the many species so small they cannot be seen without some sort of magnifying instrument. Within this hidden world are countless billions of plants and animals. For every plant or animal you can see, there are many thousands you cannot see. These microscopic organisms outnumber all other living things by so many that the number becomes difficult to imagine.

You will also discover that commonplace materials found

Adrianne, a young friend of the author's, exploring the microscopic world.

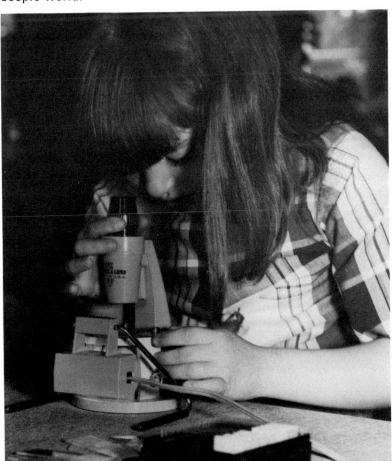

in every home reveal an unsuspected beauty of shape when viewed through a microscope. Under magnification some of these materials merely become larger. For example, the point of a pin, when viewed through a microscope, looks like a large pinpoint. Its shape or structure does not appear changed. But other materials change their form entirely when magnified. A tiny thread of green algae, for instance, is revealed to be a complicated structure whose design and detail are unsuspected until the algae is enlarged.

These microorganisms were undetected by humans until approximately three hundred years ago, when Marcello Malpighi, an Italian physician and lecturer who specialized in the study of blood circulation, invented the microscope. Malpighi's microscope was a simple device with a single lens.

While Malpighi did indeed invent the microscope, it was his contemporary Anton van Leeuwenhoek who popularized the instrument and perfected its use. Leeuwenhoek, janitor in the city hall in Delft, Holland, for most of his life, ground lenses as a hobby. Leeuwenhoek took the time and patience to grind his tiny lenses to absolute perfection. Some of them were no larger than the head of a pin, but they magnified images up to two hundred times! Leeuwenhoek ground over four hundred of these lenses during his long lifetime.

Although Leeuwenhoek was not educated as a scientist, he went about his hobby of observing objects under the microscope with all the precision and care of a true scientist. He investigated everything he could fit under one of his lenses, and wrote about and illustrated what he saw. Leeuwenhoek sent his findings to the Royal Academy of Great Britain and also to the French Academy of Science. He was elected a member of both societies.

At first people did not believe that Leeuwenhoek saw the things he said he did, but after a time they became convinced that the man was telling the truth. Many people then went to Delft to look through Leeuwenhoek's lenses. Even kings and queens stopped by to see him and to look at what he had revealed.

Our modern microscopes were developed from the simple lenses that Leeuwenhoek made. Today we have lenses that magnify objects over a thousand times, and electronic microscopes that magnify over a *hundred thousand* times. The great value of Leeuwenhoek's lenses lay in their demonstration that there really is a hidden world of living and nonliving things that few before had even suspected was there. The value of our modern lenses and instruments is in exploring this hidden world and in experimenting with microscopic organisms in order to develop new medicines, cures for diseases, and chemicals for use in industry and in food culture.

Until fairly recent times, only scientists or laboratory workers were able to explore the microscopic world. This was because microscopes are very complicated instruments and they cost a great amount of money. Now, though, small microscopes are made that are very low in cost and yet have excellent lenses that magnify clearly and easily.

The microscopes we use today are far different from the simple lenses of Anton van Leeuwenhoek. Even the simplest and least expensive of them use several lenses in groups in order to magnify and clarify the images seen through them. A lens, or a group of lenses, is mounted at the bottom of a tube. This tube is held in a support in such a manner as to be adjustable with regard to the position of the specimen. This is to say that the tube may be moved closer to or farther away from the object being examined. Adjusting the tube is called focusing the microscope, and the care with which this is done determines the accuracy and clarity of the image you see.

However, you would be unable to see any image with just the lenses at the bottom of the tube, because they are ground to provide an image in the air somewhere inside the tube. You would be unable to get your eye down inside the tube to intercept this image. So another lens, or group of lenses, is placed at the top of the tube. This top lens is made to enable you to focus on the image in the air within the tube, and also to magnify the image a little more. Now, by holding your eye close to the top of the tube, you may move the tube up or down until the magnified image of whatever is beneath the tube is brought into clear and sharp focus.

The lenses of a microscope are delicate and should never be touched with the bare fingers. They must be kept very clean, or you will be unable to focus properly and the light will be cut down so much that the image will be very dim. The best way to clean a lens of your microscope is with a lens tissue and a drop of lens-cleaning fluid. Both of these may be purchased for a few cents at optical stores, drugstores, and instrument stores. When your microscope is not being used, even for a few hours, it should be covered to protect it from the dust which is always in the air. The box it came in makes a good cover, or a large plastic bag may be pulled over the instrument.

Specimens of hundreds of different subjects are available on ready-made microscope slides. They can be bought from scientific-supply houses and school-supply stores. Your science teacher can tell you the addresses, or might even order a few slides for you. Some hobby stores sell them, and now, for a dollar or two, department and discount stores sell sets of prepared slides that provide very good specimens for examination. These sets, usually in a box containing twelve slides, are grouped by subject—biology, botany, zoology, and so on.

Slides are inexpensive enough to allow you to build up a good library of them. When you hear of a subject for study but cannot find it yourself, such as the aurelia jellyfish, you can obtain a complete set of slides at little cost. Then you can see for yourself the animal's whole life history and just how it develops. As you gain more experience and equipment, you can even take a photographic record of these things for yourself.

Make notes of what you see in a science notebook kept especially for your microscopic studies. As you progress in school you will find this notebook a very valuable aid in your learning, and if your curiosity is very strong, you will find that you will be far ahead in your science classes!

Unless you have access to a very powerful microscope, do

An old but good microscope like this one can be purchased inexpensively, and it accepts a camera attachment with no problem.

not bother with slides of bacteria. These are so small that it takes a very, very strong lens to show them to you. If you took a medium-sized bacteria species, it would take 200,000 of them touching each other to equal one inch! You would require 250 of even the very largest of the bacteria placed end to end their longest way, to make an inch.

In order to explore the hidden world, you will need some simple supplies besides your microscope. Clean, blank microscope slides, cover glasses, fine tweezers, and an eyedropper are about all you need. Microscope slides are sold in boxes at the same places where you can purchase readymade slides. Cover glasses are very thin wafers of glass used to cover the specimen on the slide to protect it from dam-

This Bausch & Lomb microprojector is perfect for someone who does a lot of photographic work. It costs about $300 without the camera.

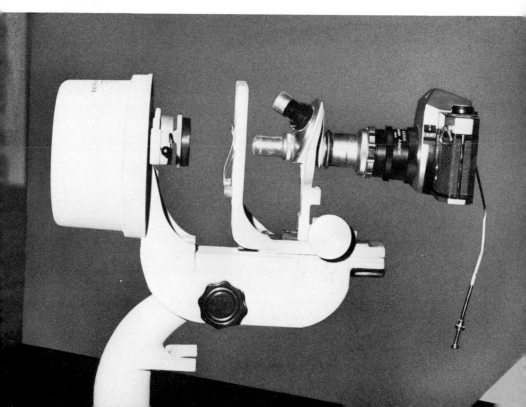

age. If you want to make a permanent mount of a slide, the cover glass is set in balsam, a very sticky fluid which hardens after being exposed to the air for a time. Balsam is sold with boxes of blank slides, or in scientific-supply houses and some school stores.

To make a permanent mount, a specimen is placed in the center of a clean, blank slide, a drop of balsam placed over the specimen, and a cover glass dropped onto the drop of balsam. A very slight pressure is placed on the cover glass to force out all air underneath it, and to spread the balsam evenly over the surface. The whole is allowed to stand for several days until the balsam hardens, after which time it is ready for use. A slide made up in this manner will last for many years, and the specimen within the balsam will be perfectly preserved. Any school science teacher can show you how to make up permanent mounts.

For temporary mounts, just to watch an animal or other specimen, the cover glass can be held in place on the slide by touching the tip of a toothpick dipped in Vaseline to the cover glass to act as glue. The Vaseline will hold the cover securely to the slide while you are using it.

In order to watch the animals in a drop of pond water you must have some way to hold the drop of water in place, yet keep it from evaporating. Slides are available which have a hollow area ground into them. They are called cavity slides, hanging-drop slides, or sometimes well slides. A cavity slide can be made very easily by fastening a washer on to the slide with a bit of epoxy cement and allowing the cement to harden completely before using the slide. When you use a cavity slide, the drop of water containing the animals from the pond is placed in the center of a cover glass which has had a line of Vaseline placed all around for adhesive. Put the drop of water on the same side of the cover glass as the Vaseline. Now place the microscope slide on top of the cover glass so that the drop of water comes within the cavity in the slide or the hole of the washer if you are using a homemade cavity slide. Press the slide down to glue the cover glass in place with the Vaseline; then lift up the whole assembly and quickly turn it over so the cover glass is on top. You must turn it quickly so that the drop of water does not run off to the side and then all around the slide or the washer, instead of remaining on the cover glass. The animals in the drop of water will live for many hours while you watch them.

This book will give you a hint of the endless variety of objects that may be observed under the microscope. Some of them are alive. Others are not. The important thing to remember is that anything at all is likely to have something on it or in it that is invisible to your eyes without the aid of a magnifying lens or microscope. With the help of one of the very low-priced instruments like the Bausch and Lomb Elementary School Microscopes and a guide such as this book, you can begin to explore the microscopic world. All you need besides these items is curiosity.

2

A New Look at Some Familiar Objects

LET US NOW TAKE A LOOK AT SOME OF THE MARVELS OF THE hidden world. The things we will look at are things that you can find quite easily. We can start with some things that can be found around the house.

For many hundreds of years the only fibers used by man were natural plant fibers, like flax from which linen cloth is made, cotton, or silk from the cocoons made by a moth. Man had to use these fibers in whatever condition he found them in nature. With the exception of silk, which was many hundreds of feet long, most of the fibers were short and had to be spun into yarn before being used. The fibers were uneven in size, and the material made from them was rougher than some of our modern fabrics.

Silk fibers are so fine that many of them have to be twisted together to make a single thread. From this thread, cloth is woven on huge looms. The stockings women used to wear were woven from silk thread. The reason I say *used* to wear is because very few real silk stockings are worn today. We have learned to make better fibers for stockings.

Perhaps your mother, sister, or a relative has an old silk stocking you may use. If so, stretch a part of it loosely over the microscope's stage, the small platform just below the tube containing the lenses, and examine it. See the intricate way it is woven, and notice the looseness of the twisted fibers. If you cannot find a silk stocking, examine a piece of silk sewing thread or a ravel from silk fabric.

In recent years man has learned to make fibers by chemical processes. These are called synthetic fibers, and they have very nearly replaced the natural fibers in many cases. Today almost all the stockings worn by women are made out of a synthetic fiber called nylon, instead of silk.

Look at a regular nylon stocking under your instrument. You will see that the threads are smoother and more even than those making the silk stocking you just looked at. The nylon stocking is woven the same way as a silk stocking, but in the nylon one the threads are a little heavier and a lot smoother.

The next photograph is also a nylon stocking. This one is woven a little differently from the ordinary one. This is a run-resistant stocking, and if you examine the photograph closely, you will see that there is a locking stitch every once in a while. This stocking is very thin and fragile. It was woven from a single nylon fiber instead of a bundle of twisted fibers. See the smooth, shiny fibers? The dull part of each loop is where the stocking was worn against the leg, and the fiber has become roughened a little bit in those places. There are two locking stitches in this picture. Can you find them?

The last photograph of a nylon stocking is one of a sup-

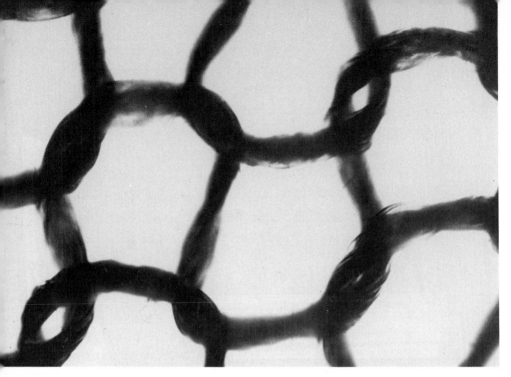

The strands of a silk stocking are not as smooth as they appear to the naked eye.

Notice how much more regular the strands of this nylon stocking are than those of the silk stocking.

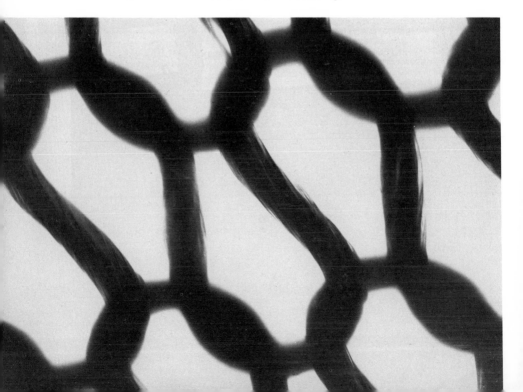

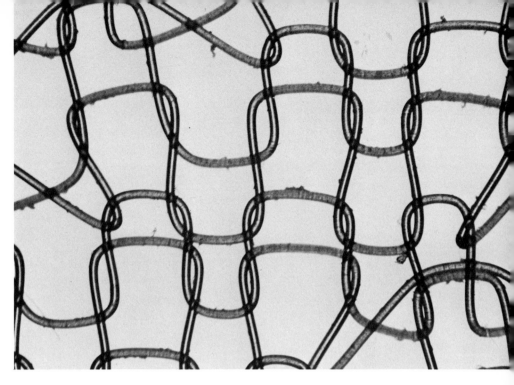

You can plainly see two of the run-locking stitches in this run-resistant weave of a nylon stocking.

The heavy black "coil-spring" in this support-weave nylon stocking is what gives support to the leg.

port stocking. Here you can see the regular weave of the base stocking, together with the heavy, twisted, springy strand woven through the stocking. This resilient strand is stretched tightly around the leg when the stocking is worn, giving support to the muscles of the wearer.

Look at this photograph and see if you can identify the fibers. They are animal fibers. They are human hairs. Note the short, thick one near the center of the photograph. This strand shows clearly that hair is hollow, like a pipe.

Hair is quite fine, the average strand being about 5/1000 of an inch in diameter! Girls' hair is sometimes finer than boys'. Usually the hair on your arm or leg is finer than that on your head. Try looking at differently colored hair. Look at hair from different parts of your body. The coarsest hair comes from a man's face where he shaves every day, or from

Did you know that your hairs are little hollow tubes?

a beard or moustache, because this hair has been cut off almost every day when the man shaves. This constant cutting makes the hair grow stiffer and coarser.

Most animal hair is very nearly like human hair. Sheep's hair is different, however. This is the fiber from which we make wool yarn. Look at a strand of wool and you will see that each hair is made up of overlapping plates.

Hair is composed of a horny material called keratin. Animal horns and fingernails are also made of keratin. Most hair is hollow, and the hollow contains air and pigment, which makes the hair appear to be colored black, brown, red, or shades of these colors. It is true that keratin is an albuminoid, which is a protein, but hair does not "lose" protein when washed or exposed to the sun, and this protein cannot be "put back" into the hair by the use of any shampoos.

Salt and sugar crystals look almost alike. Sprinkle just a few grains of sugar on a clean microscope slide and look at them. The irregularly shaped grains are crystals that were either broken up into small pieces or melted together. Not all the crystals are the same shape. All of them are broken one way or another when the sugar is granulated into nearly uniform-sized grains.

After examining the dry sugar, with an eyedropper place a tiny drop of water on top of the sugar to dissolve it. Then allow the sugar water to dry and look at it again. How do the crystals differ?

Now sprinkle a few grains of table salt on a clean slide and look at them. Salt belongs to the group of minerals having cubic crystalline structure. This means that the natural shape of a salt crystal is a cube.

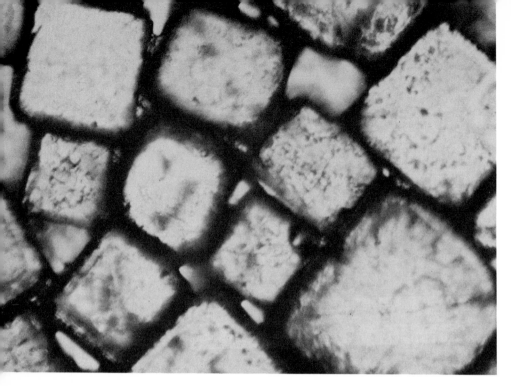

See the cubic structure of these salt crystals? If you crush them, they will fracture into smaller cubes.

Notice how these sugar crystals are all rough and broken as compared with salt crystals.

These iodine crystals have formed in the puddle of alcohol in which they were dissolved.

These are Epsom salts, or magnesium sulphate crystals.

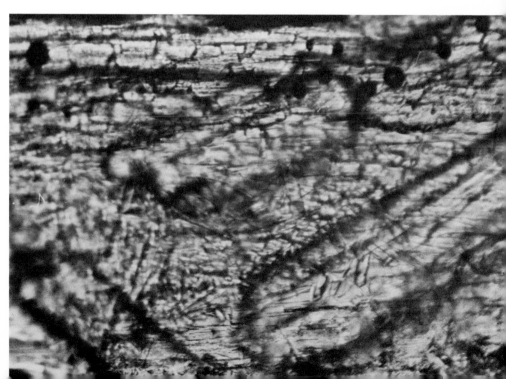

The surface of each salt cube might be roughened a bit. This is because the cubes were tumbled about in the shaker or container. The sides are flat, however. The cubes having rounded corners got that way from tumbling during the refining process.

Salt is mined from deposits sometimes miles deep. Of all the hundreds of things human beings eat, salt is the only one that was never alive in one form or another! Everything else was alive either as a plant or as an animal. The chemical composition of salt is sodium chloride. Sodium is a reactive metal, which means that it reacts very easily with other elements. The gas is chlorine, one of the deadly gases used in World War I. When equal amounts of chlorine and sodium combine, both parts become harmless to man, and combine to form cubic crystals of table salt.

Salt is one of the most important minerals on earth. Without it, animals and humans could not exist. Without salt man would die because salt helps maintain the delicate chemical balance in our bodies. In ancient times salt was so valuable that it was used for money. In the Roman army the men were paid partly in money, and partly in salt! The Roman word for salt was *Sal*, and the salt payment was called *salarium*. Through the years since then, *salarium* came to be called *salary*. Your mother and father may work for their salary. In ancient times, part of their take-home pay would have been blocks of hard salt!

While you are looking at crystals, go into the bathroom and find the bottle of iodine in the medicine cabinet. Put a tiny drop of this solution in the center of a slide and place it on the microscope. You will see only a faintly brown spot. Continue to watch, though, and soon you will notice some changes in the drop. It will start to turn darker in places, and begin to look rough.

Suddenly, almost like magic, crystals will start to grow before your eyes, until they zoom up so rapidly that you instinctively draw back from the instrument. The crystals appear as though they are going to jump right out of the lens at you!

These are the crystals of iodine. They formed as the alcohol, in which they were dissolved to make the tincture of iodine used for disinfecting cuts, evaporated in the air. As a matter of fact, you will see some of the alcohol still remaining around the crystal cluster, and as you watch this will slowly evaporate, leaving the iodine crystals standing high and dry. The photograph shows the rim of alcohol around the crystals growing out of it.

Iodine is an important part of our diet. Each person needs a certain amount of iodine in his body. Iodine is known to prevent goiter, the enlargement of the thyroid gland, and is sometimes used in the treatment of that disease.

Iodine is poisonous if taken internally, so it should always be kept carefully labeled and out of the reach of children.

Seaweed is rich in iodine. If you taste a piece of seaweed, it tastes very bitter. Walk along a beach on a sunny afternoon and step on the patches of seaweed cast up by the waves. The air is filled with the acrid smell of iodine.

You can make still another crystal for examination. Have you ever hurt your hand or foot and soaked it in Epsom salts dissolved in hot water? The chemical name for Epsom salts is magnesium sulphate. It is used much in industry. In the home it is mainly used as a laxative, or to relieve pain in swollen hands or feet.

A few crystals of the chemical in a tiny drop of water on your slide will grow into natural crystalline shapes as the water evaporates. These crystals are usually long, rodlike shapes. These can be seen against the background of dissolved chemical in the photograph.

After having examined these four different types of crystals, you might compare them to each other to note the differences of structure. Here you have an easy look at the way minerals crystallize.

Have you a raw potato in the kitchen? With a razor blade, try to slice off a very thin section, a slice so thin that you can see through it. You can do this by resting a small piece of the potato on a small piece of glass, a small sheet of metal, or a slicing block from the kitchen and holding the potato tightly against the edge of the glass while drawing the razor blade through the potato. As soon as you have cut off the top of the potao, move the potato up a hair's breadth and make another slice. A little practice will enable you to make very thin cuts. This is the principle of the slicing instrument called a microtome, which is used to obtain tissue-thin slices of subjects for study.

Lay the slice of potato on a slide and look at it through the highest power lens you have. You will see many rounded cells all through the potato. These are starch grains. Starch is broken down into sugar during the digestive process, and then the sugar is rapidly consumed by the body to provide energy. That sugar which is not immediately used is stored by the body in the form of fat.

If you have difficulty seeing the grains of starch, a tiny drop of iodine placed on the slice will stain the starch grains blue. Then, after the iodine has been on the slice for a minute or two, it can be rinsed off with a drop of water. Now the starch grains stand out plainly.

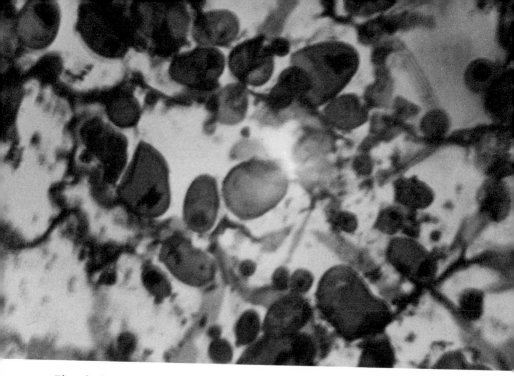

The darker, rounded spots are starch within the potato. Iodine was applied to the potato so the starch grains would show clearly in the photograph.

Each speck in this photograph is a whole colony of yeast bacteria!

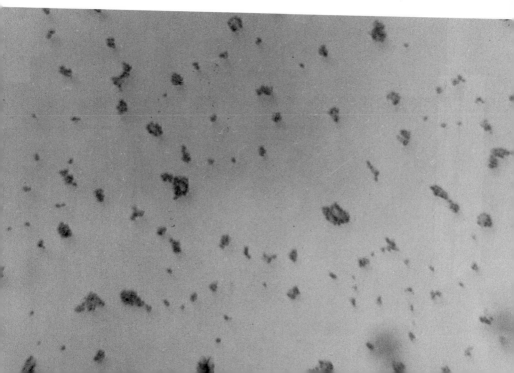

Have you ever baked bread? If so, you must have used a bacteria called yeast in order to make the dough rise. Bread rises because the yeast makes gas which fills the dough with millions of tiny bubbles, blowing the dough up just like a balloon!

Yeast is also used in the fermentation of beer. For many years men brewed beer without even knowing what it was that made the mixture of malt, hops, and water turn into an alcoholic beverage. Now it is known that the yeast in the mixture consumes the sugar and replaces it with alcohol; and when all the sugar is replaced with the alcohol, the beer is ready to drink. Yeast also puts the fizz in homemade rootbeer.

Yeast is one of the causes of food spoilage. It contains chemical substances called enzymes, which break down the food structure and cause it to decompose, or rot.

Yeast is another important component of the human diet, for it contains the vitamins thiamine and niacin. Niacin is one of the vitamins that helps prevent pellagra, and thiamine is a preventative for beriberi.

Yeast is so small that it is difficult to get a clear picture of it through a low-powered microscope. The yeast particles shown in the photograph are really clusters of individual bacteria.

Have you ever had a piece of bread become moldy? Perhaps it was lying forgotten someplace, or maybe during the hot summer a slice was left loose in the breadbox, and it became covered in spots with black mold. This mold is a parasitic plant called a fungus, and the black part is the sporebearing part, just like the mushrooms popping up in your lawn are the sporebearers of that particular kind of fungus.

The name of the black bread mold is *Rhizopus nigra-cans*, and it is a very interesting growth. First the plant sends tiny threads through the bread. These are the roots of the fungus. There are two strains, or sexes, of roots. Whenever two of these come together, they fuse and form a black sporehead called a zygote.

Under a powerful microscope lens you can plainly see the fusing of two of the threadlike roots and the forming of the zygote. The round, black zygotes each contain many thousands of tiny spores. On the bread, to the naked eye, these look like black dust.

Oranges and other citrus fruits also make a black mold very like the one on a slice of bread. The mold forms first on a bruise spot on the skin.

The black balls are the spores of the fungus. Each ball may contain hundreds of thousands of spores!

3

The Animal World

ANOTHER INTERESTING SUBJECT FOR STUDY UNDER THE MI-croscope is an organism called *Pediculus humanus capitus*, more commonly known as a louse or cootie. This organism is a parasitic insect that lives on the bodies, usually the head, of warm-blooded animals. These lice spread typhus and other diseases, some of which are fatal to humans. During wars and in prison camps, where people cannot keep clean, these diseases spread, killing thousands at a time.

Modern hygiene has virtually eliminated these insects, but a prepared slide of this animal may be purchased from most school-laboratory-supply companies.

Lice live by piercing the skin on the head and sucking blood. The claws on their feet fold back tightly against the rest of the foot. If you look closely at the foot, you will see

A head louse.

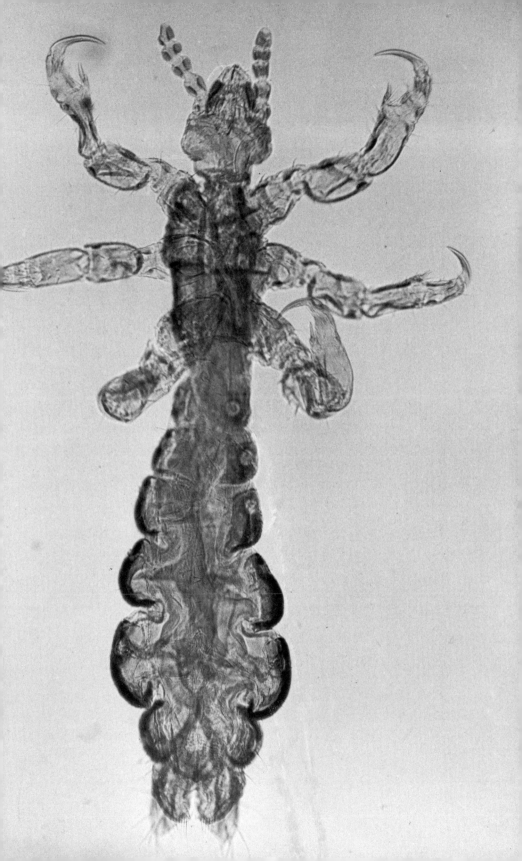

that there is a small curve at the base of the claw. When the claw is folded back, one hair is caught in this curved area and clamped tightly with the claw. By catching a hair in each of its six claws, the louse can hold on to the head very well, and it is almost impossible to dislodge it by scratching.

The eggs, or nits, of the louse are fastened to the hairs. Lice hatch their eggs in an unusual manner. The shells have a kind of trapdoor on the upper end. When ready to hatch, the baby louse gulps air and forces it through its body. Finally enough pressure is formed at the bottom of the eggshell literally to blow the baby louse out through the trapdoor!

Another insect which has hooks on its feet is the *Bombyx mori*, or silkworm moth. The Chinese started cultivating these insects over five thousand years ago, and now the moth would be unable to survive in the wild state. The caterpillars are fed mulberry leaves and just sit in straw trays until they are ready to spin their cocoons. The pupae are killed after the cocoon is spun so that the adult moth

The large hooked feet of the silkworm moth enable the insect to walk on almost any surface.

does not emerge. If it did, it would eat a hole in the cocoon to get out, thereby ruining the cocoon for silk production. By killing the pupa within each cocoon, the silk can be unreeled in one endless strand, which may be up to five miles in length! A single strand of silk is so fine that it is difficult to see it, but it is stronger than a strand of steel the same size!

Prepared slides of the various stages of development of this insect are available from the Japan Trade Center in New York City.

Do you have a cat or dog? Watch him closely, and you will see him scratch himself every so often with one of his feet. The reason he itches is probably because he has fleas. Almost all dogs and most cats have fleas living on their skins.

If you are very sharp-eyed and fast, you can catch a flea when the dog starts to scratch. Look at the exact spot his claws are scratching, then quickly pull the hairs aside and continue to search the spot. The flea will try to hide in the hair next to where you are looking, so be quick.

When you find one, catch it between your fingertips and squeeze it just a little bit. You want to stun the animal, not squash it flat. Place it on a slide and drop a cover glass over it in case it revives and tries to jump away.

The photograph shows a dog flea. You can plainly see the proboscis, the long, tubelike mouth part which the flea sticks into the dog's skin and through which it sucks the blood of the animal.

Daphnids are called water fleas, and they do resemble fleas a little, hopping around in the water like fleas hop in the air. Daphnids are found in ponds which have a lot of algae and other foods in them. Very clean, clear ponds do

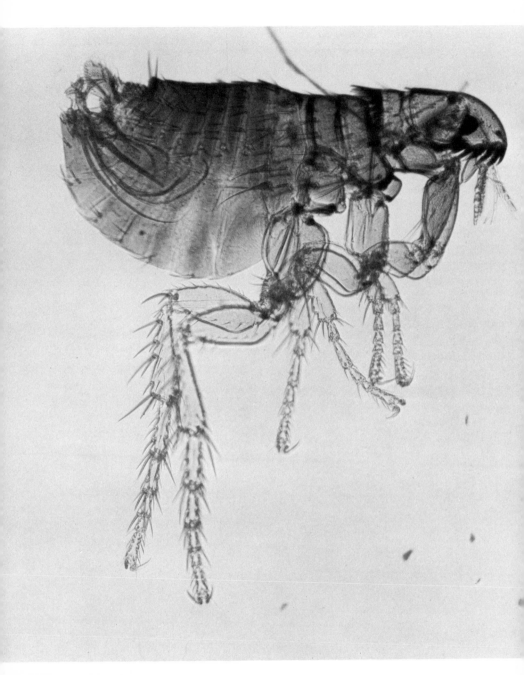

This dog flea can jump for great distances by snapping its long hind legs.

not usually contain daphnids. Sometimes you may see a red cloud in the water of a slightly muddy pond. The cloud is composed of millions of daphnids. If you have an aquarium of tropical fish, or even goldfish, a netful of these little animals will be wonderful food for your pets. If you cannot find daphnids in the wild, your pet store will usually have them for sale in small containers.

Another good live food for pet fish is brine shrimp, little animals that live in salt water. They breed by countless billions and lay eggs in such quantity that they are gathered in shovels. The eggs wash ashore and pile up in great drifts.

A strange thing about brine-shrimp eggs is that they can be dried out completely, yet when they are put back in warm salt water they will hatch in a few hours! Eggs of brine shrimp have been kept dry for *fifty years* and have still hatched when put back into water!

It is easier to buy a quarter's worth of fully grown brine shrimp at the pet store than it is to raise your own. But if you are interested in seeing how they hatch, you can buy small bottles of eggs at any pet store and hatch them according to the directions on the label.

When the shrimp first hatch, they do not look like the one in the photograph, which is an adult brine shrimp. The baby shrimp, called *nauplii*, are little triangular animals with two feet that kick out like oars when they swim. Baby brine shrimp are excellent food for baby tropical fish.

To look at a brine shrimp while it is still alive, pick up one with an eyedropper and drop it onto a cover glass. Then stick a cavity slide or a slide with a washer glued to it to make a "cavity" over the cover glass with a bit of Vaseline to seal it. Invert the slide and you can watch your brine shrimp swim around in the drop of water for a long time.

While you were out looking at daphnids in the pond, you may have been bitten by a mosquito. The mosquito has a long proboscis which it pushes through your skin in order to suck your blood. While it is sucking the blood, it is injecting saliva into you to keep your blood from clotting in its proboscis. It is this saliva that makes you itch.

The mosquito's saliva sometimes carries disease germs of malaria, yellow fever, and many other dreadful sicknesses.

Mosquitoes have killed millions of people all over the world with the germs they carry, so it is a good idea to swat every mosquito you see.

While you are still looking at insects, find a bee. If you must kill one to look at it, use a fly swatter; but be careful not to smash it flat, because you want a wing in one piece. Put the wing on a slide and examine it all over.

See how it is constructed of a thin film stretched over strengthening veins. The short, pointed hairs growing all over the wing are sensory hairs.

A most interesting thing about a bee's wing is the spiral hinge at the leading edge of the rear wing. If you were careful taking the wing off, you can see this spiral very clearly. Its purpose is to act as a lock when the insect flies. When the wings are in flight position, this spiral locks into a flap on the forewing, thus hooking the two wings together to make a wide surface for supporting the body of the bee.

While you are searching for a bee, the chances are that you will also find a moth. You do not have to kill a moth to get some of the scales from a wing. Just hold the wings carefully pinched together, while you scrape off a tiny spot with the point of a needle. Scrap the scales off the needle onto the surface of a clean slide and drop a cover glass on top to keep them from blowing away.

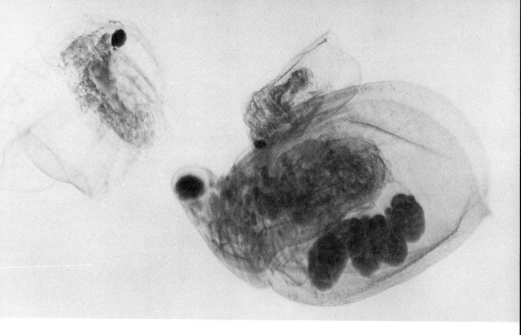

These daphnia, called water fleas, hop about in the water just like fleas.

An adult brine shrimp.

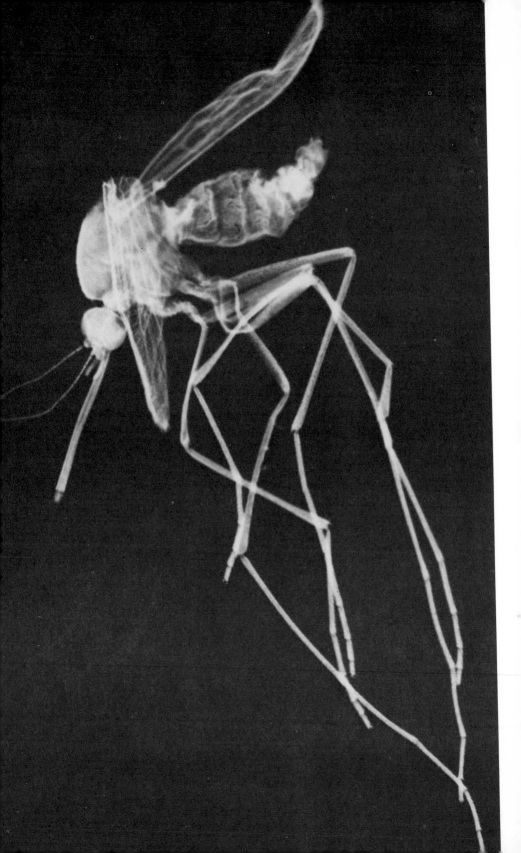

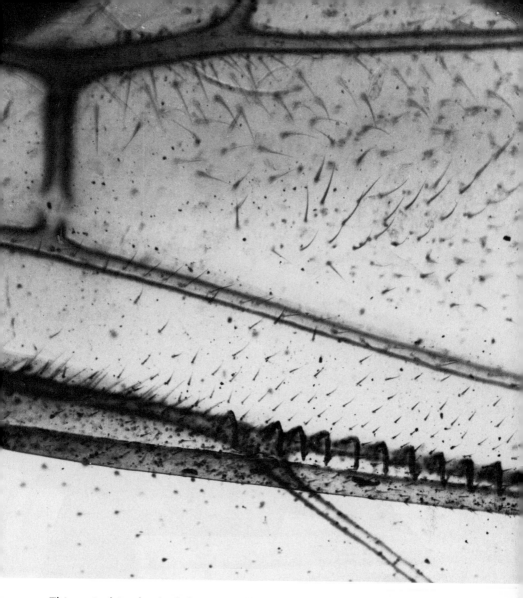

This spiral is the lock between the bee's front and hind wings which holds the two wings together when the bee is in flight.

The mosquito has a very efficient proboscis for sucking your blood.

Look at the scales and see if you can identify the different shapes, which vary according to the area of the wing on which they are found. The flat, leaflike scales are out in the wide or flat area of the wing. The long, slender scales come from nearer the body of the moth, and the long, fine, hairlike scales are at the joint of the wing and the body. They are the scales that look like a fur cape on the "shoulder" of the moth.

While some moths and some butterflies have scales that appear colored, many of these scales are actually clear. The brilliant color on the wings of the insects, called prismatic

Notice the different shapes of these moth scales, which come from different parts of the insect's body.

coloring, is caused by the light reflecting through the wings from different angles. The scientific term for this is refraction of light.

For the next experiment you will need a dead goldfish. Goldfish die frequently in pet shops, and the owner of your local shop will be happy to give you one. If none are available when you ask, ask him to save one for you.

Now, place the dead goldfish on a paper towel and pick off a scale with a sharp needle. If you need a magnifying glass to do so, ask someone to hold the fish for you so you can easily pick the scale.

The transparent scale of a goldfish.

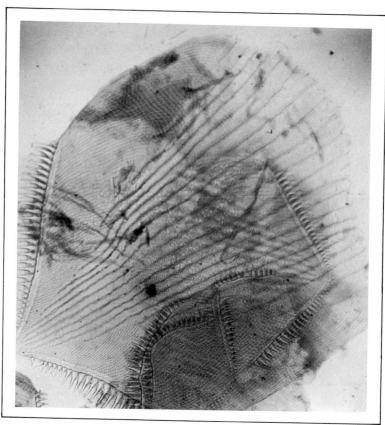

Place the scale on a slide and cover it with a cover glass. When you look at it through the microscope, you will be amazed at how beautiful the scale is.

Look around your fruit bowl on the table. You may see, especially in the hot summer months, tiny flies buzzing around the fruit. Bananas especially attract these fruit flies, which are called drosophila.

Catch one, and put one of the wings on a slide, held down with a cover glass. Like the bee's wing, this one is made of a thin film stretched over stiff veins and covered with fine, short, stiff hairs. The vein all around the front or leading edge of the wing is very much stiffer and larger than the other veins in the center of the wing. This leading vein, called the costa, or costal vein, stiffens the front edge of the wing and supports it along its length.

When an insect like a fly or butterfly or moth is first born, its wings are all crumpled up and wet and soft. The first thing the animal must do is expand and dry its wings. Otherwise it could not fly.

Inside the body of the newly emerged insect is a fluid which is pumped into the veins of the wings. In a large moth just emerging from the cocoon, you can see very plainly the body of the insect pumping the fluid out into the wings. With each pump of the body the wings expand a little more, until finally they are fully expanded and the veins are all full of the fluid.

Now the insect fans its wings to dry them. As it does so, the fluid in the veins dries and hardens. This stiffens the veins to act as ribs which hold the wings in position. Then the insect expels the remaining fluid from its body in a squirt, and it is ready to fly off.

A fruit fly is a little too small for you to work with for the following examination, so swat a horsefly or even an ordinary housefly just enough to kill it.

Place the fly under a strong magnifying glass and pick off a section of one of the big eyes with a fine, stiff needle. Place this section flat on a clean slide, covering it with a cover glass.

Now look at it under the microscope. You are looking at what is called a compound eye. Many insects and some crustaceans—lobsters, crawfish, shrimp, crabs—have this kind of eye. There are hundreds of individual lenses, called ommatidia, in a single compound eye. The insect having such eyes sees things as a pattern of small dots. Look at a photograph in the newspaper under your magnifying glass. You will see that it is not made up of dark and light areas at all, but of hundreds or thousands of tiny black dots of varying sizes. This is very much like the way an insect with

The entire wing of a fruit fly is covered with stiff, tiny hairs.

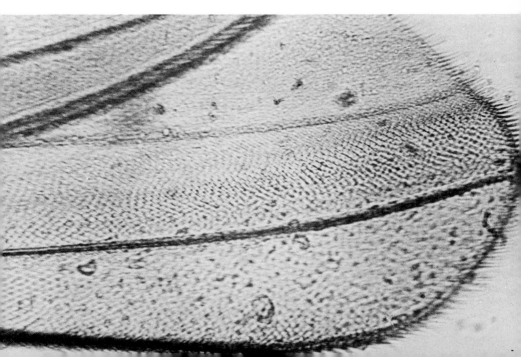

The ommatidia, or lenses, of a fly's eye. Flies see things as a series of dots rather than the whole image we see.

This lizard's skin looks as though it were woven out of threads.

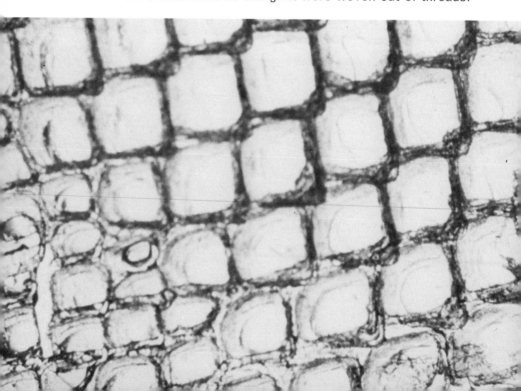

compound eyes sees everything, as a pattern of dots instead of patches of color.

An interesting pattern that you can observe under your microscope is that of a flake of skin from any reptile. All reptiles shed their skins at intervals. If you have a pet lizard, or one of the little green anoles which are incorrectly called chameleons and which are sold by the thousands in every pet shop and most five-and-ten-cent stores, save a piece of the skin and examine it.

What does the pattern remind you of? Think back a bit, but if you can't remember, look again at the picture of the silk or nylon stocking. The thickened edges of the scales on the reptile's skin look just as though they were woven like the stocking. The clear squares of skin within the thick edges are soft and flexible, and allow the animal to move quickly and without effort. If the skin were stiff, it would hamper the movements of the reptile.

If you have a canary or parakeet, save a feather when one falls off and look at the delicate structure through the lens.

This photograph is of a hackle feather of a canary. The hackle feathers are usually long and thin and cover the back of the neck. These feathers are very flexible so that they bend easily, allowing the bird to move its head around without the feathers hampering it. Since these hackle feathers do not help the bird in flight, it is not necessary for the barbs, the hairlike strands growing from the central rib of the feather, to be held together to form a web to hold air.

Now let us look at another kind of feather—a contour feather from the breast of a barred owl.

Contour feathers, like hackle feathers, do not help a bird in flight, but are merely the shaping and insulating feathers that cover the bodies of birds. There are many ribs to each

contour feather, instead of a single, central shaft, and the barbs grow from both sides of the ribs. As the barbs project from the ribs, they overlap to form an air-entrapping mesh, which makes a wonderful insulation for the bird and keeps it warm in the winter cold.

You can easily recognize a contour feather from a bird by the curved shape and the fact that at the base the feather is very fluffy and puffed up, while the outer end is flat and smooth.

(Left) These contour feathers of an owl are soft and downy to act as insulation and to shape the bird.

A hackle feather of a canary. These feathers can be open in structure because they do not aid the bird in flight.

The Plant World

PLANTS ARE FASCINATING SUBJECTS FOR MICROSCOPIC STUDY when taken apart and examined in detail.

A leaf, root, or stem is too thick to examine under the microscope unless you are able to slice sections so thin that light may penetrate them. Otherwise, it will be better to purchase a few commercial slides to examine.

Roots are, in many ways, the most important part of a plant. They perform three major functions necessary for the welfare of the plant. One is feeding the part of the plant that grows above ground by sending up water and minerals absorbed from the soil in which it is growing. Another is storing nourishment to feed the plant over the winter. A third function is to anchor the plant firmly into the ground.

The amazing thing about roots is the speed of their

growth. The fine, hairlike thread roots (sometimes called hair roots) may grow so rapidly that they increase by inches in a matter of an hour or so! What makes this even more amazing is the fact that these hairs, so tender that the slightest touch will break them, must force their way through hard soil, over, under, and around rocks and pebbles, and through sand, clay, or dirt. The roots are attracted to moisture found between the particles of soil, sucking it all up and sending it on its way up into the plant above ground.

It is possible for the thread root to do all this because it has on its very tip a hard cap of special cells. This cap is extremely tough and wear resistant, and is constantly being replenished with new cells as it wears away. Behind this tip the root is covered with very fine hairs which suck up moisture.

The cap of an onion root is the hardest part, enabling the root to penetrate the hardest of soils.

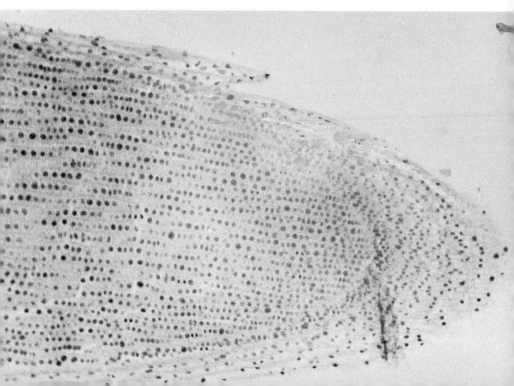

In this photograph of a lengthwise section of the tip of an onion root, this cap can be distinguished by the arrangement of its cells. While the cells in the root proper are all arranged in even rows, those of the cap appear in a helter-skelter pattern, and are surrounded by a tough, outer layer of root cells.

Two other very popular slides are those of the root and the stem of the Tilia tree, commonly known as the lime tree, or basswood. You will see that the root is different from the stem when you examine them together. In our photographs of the two cross-sections you may make this comparison. The outside ring of root cells is called the epidermis, which means "outer skin." The next band of cells is the cortex. After that you can see the endodermis—the skin within, or the inner skin. Following the endodermis is the layer of phloem and xylem cells, and then the pith center.

Xylem cells transfer water and minerals from the ground up into the trunk, branches, and leaves of the tree. The leaves then convert the water and minerals into sugar by a complex process called photosynthesis. Then the phloem cells carry the sugar down to the pith and cortex of the roots, where it is stored for the next year's growth.

Now look at the photograph of a cross-section of a *Tilia* stem. The small central area is the pith. Surrounding this is a wide area with radiating lines and dark rings in it. The lines are the medullary rays of the tree, and the rings are growth rings. How old would you say this stem was when it was cut to make this slide? By counting the dark rings within the inner area, you can see that it was six years old. The white circles are the xylem cells. These are larger in the spring growth wood, which is nearest the center of the stem

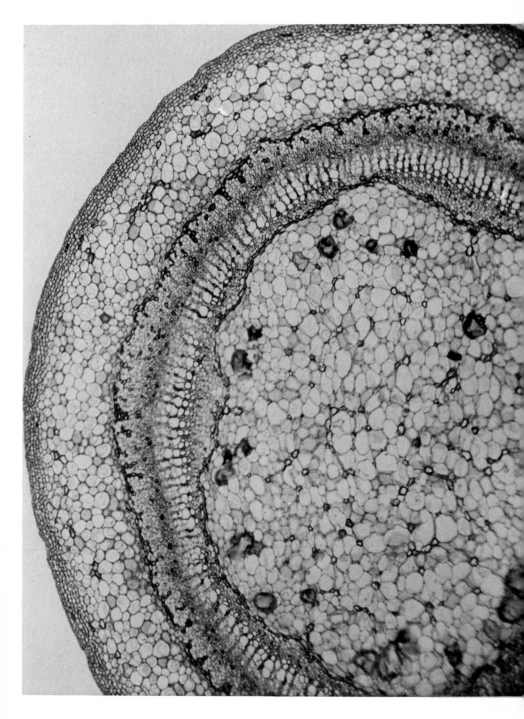

A cross-section of a Tilia root. Each root is made up of thousands of long cells.

A cross-section of a Tilia stem. Compare the shape and arrangement of the cells to those of the root.

at each growth ring, than they are in the summer or fall wood. The dark ring enclosing the growth-ring area is called the cambium layer. This layer, only one cell thick, is so thin that you would have to look very closely to find it in a small stem. The cambium layer is the growth layer of a tree. Its cells rapidly reproduce, causing the trunk of the tree to grow in width. The cambium layer also produces the next layer of cells, the phloem cells, but these are manufactured much more slowly than the xylem cells.

A leaf, which looks like a piece of rough green paper in your hand, becomes a very complicated structure when examined under a powerful microscope.

When you look at most leaves, you will see that the veins follow a definite pattern. Either they run in straight lines from the top to the bottom of the leaf, as in grass, wheat, and orchid leaves, for example; or the leaf has a central vein from which the smaller ones branch out on both sides.

The leaf of one plant, though, has veins that do not follow a pattern at all, but run every which way inside the leaf. This is the ivy. Pick an ivy leaf and put it into water to let the body of the leaf blade rot away. Look at it every few days, because as soon as the leaf body has softened and loosened, you should wash it away from the veins which remain. The veins of ivy are very hard and tough, so you can boil the leaf for a time to hasten the softening process, if you like. Now look at the veins through the microscope. They look like a small vine, tangled and crooked.

Almost every plant or flower releases pollen, tiny grains found in the part of the flower called the anther. Plants are usually fertilized by an insect that, while walking about on the flower in search of nectar, brushes the pollen from the

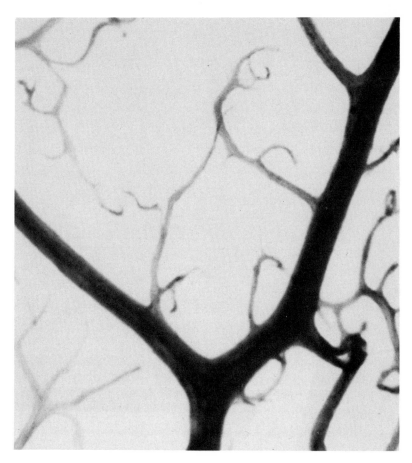

The veins of an ivy leaf.

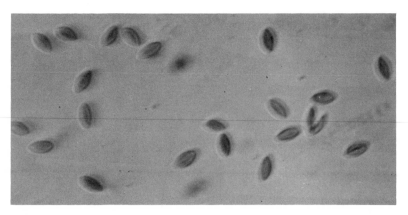

The pollen of each plant has a distinctive shape. This pollen is from a maple tree.

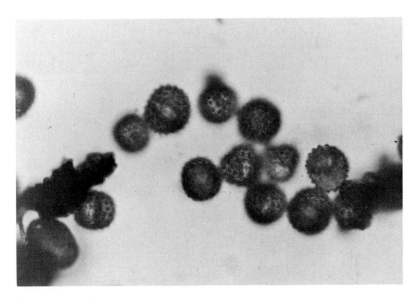

Ragweed pollen.

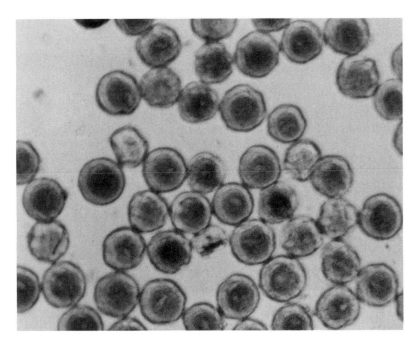

Some of these crocus pollen grains have started to develop.

anther of one flower and then carries it to the stigma of another flower. There it germinates in the sticky, sugary nectar. Then a tiny tube grows and penetrates the length of the stigma to the ovary. In the ovary the embryo seeds are fertilized and develop into ripe seeds.

Trees and many other plants spill their pollen into the air, where it is blown around by the wind. Some of the windblown pollen is sure to land on another tree of the same species and fertilize it to make seeds.

Hay fever is caused by inhaling the pollen of ragweeds and other plants. If you get hay fever, it is said that you have an allergy to the pollen causing the trouble. As you can see in the photograph, grains of ragweed pollen resemble globes studded with spikes.

Pollen is a fascinating material. Each species of plant has a different kind of pollen. People who study pollen are able to identify the plant from which it comes by the shape and size of the grains of pollen. Pollen grains from a poplar tree, for instance, are exactly the same size and shape as the pollen grains from every other poplar tree in the world.

Life in a
Drop of Water

NOW YOU CAN GO ON A FIELD TRIP. YOU WILL NEED A SMALL
bottle which you can close tightly, a dipper of some kind—
a ladle, a cup, or even a small pan with a handle—and a
paper bag to put the bottle into to keep it out of strong
sunlight.

With this equipment, you can go to any small lake or
pond and discover a wonderful source of animals for microscopic study. A pond in a field is a good source, especially if
it has green algae growing in it. You can identify the algae
because it looks like green hair, or slime, or patches of
green, cottony matter. Stagnant water is even better. A
puddle that has been filled with water for several days or
even the wet drainage ditches running parallel to many
roads have many species of microorganisms living in them.

With your dipper, dip up a scoop of water from near the

bottom of the pond (or puddle, or whatever), getting a little of the bottom mud too, but not too much. Pick out a small pinch of the green algae and drop it into the bottle: then fill the bottle with the water you scooped out. Seal it tightly so it will not leak, and drop it into the paper bag. Then head for home and your microscope.

You have put an entire world of hundreds, maybe even thousands, of living animals and plants into that little bottle. The tiny animals are called protozoa, from the Greek words *proto*, which means "before" or "first," and *zoa*, which means "animal." It is believed that all life on the earth evolved from the first protozoan animals. You may discover some larger animals, too, when you start to examine the water.

Earlier in this book you learned how to make a cavity slide, and how to use it. You will need it now to examine the organisms found in the drop of pond water. Put a drop on your cavity slide and place the slide on the stage of the microscope. Adjust the light and focus the lens carefully, watching all the time until the specks in the water come into sharp focus.

Perhaps you will first see some fairly large, beautiful, pink- or rose-colored animals swimming about very rapidly. Watch them for a time. These animals, called Blepharisma, belong to a group of protozoans called ciliates. These ciliates have short hairs, called cilia, on their bodies which they can wave rapidly to help them move about. Belpharisma eat smaller protozoa and tiny plant life.

Probably the greatest number of living things you will see in the drop of water are tiny, long creatures which move very rapidly in a strange revolving motion. These ciliates are called rotifers because they travel in a revolving, spiral

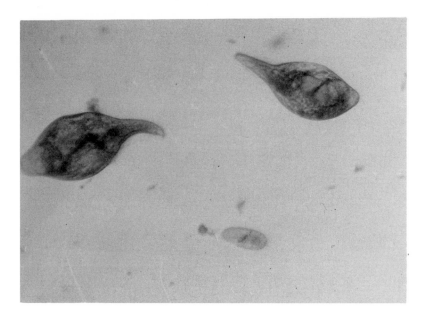

These Blepharisma are some of the most beautifully colored protozoa.

These rotifers travel through the water in a revolving motion.

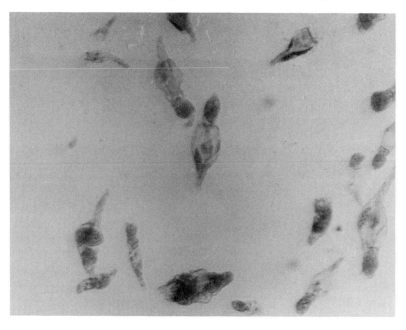

path, forced ahead by the oarlike action of their cilia.

Rotifers come in a great number of shapes. As a rule, a mass of these rotifers, known as a colony, will be all the same shape. The rotifers are usually found in stagnant water rather than fresh, clean water. Rotifers are valuable as food for larger protozoa.

A strange creature might ooze up from a little of the mud you collected. It is one of the larger protozoa, and is sometimes so large that it can be seen with the naked eye. It

This species of amoeba is so big that a sharp eye may detect one in the water without the aid of a microscope.

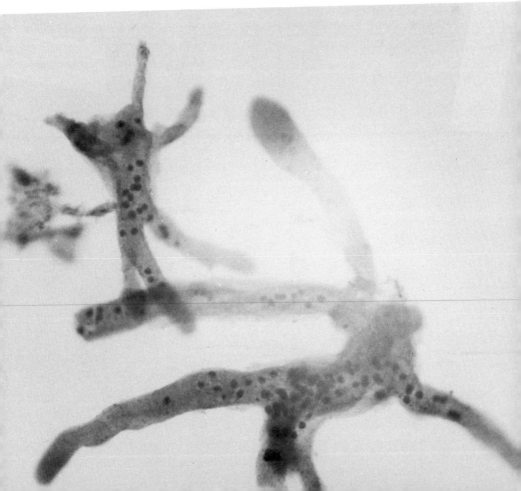

moves along slowly by pushing out a portion of its body, then pulling the rest of its body after it. This animal is known as an amoeba, from a Greek word meaning "to change shape." And that is exactly what an amoeba is always doing.

If you watch one long enough, you may see the unique way an amoeba eats. The animal merely flows up to its food, wraps its body around the particle of food, and closes over the opening, leaving the food inside itself ready for digesting!

One of the first animals studied in biology classes is the paramecium, sometimes called the slipper animalcule (another term for a microscopic organism, meaning "little animal") because it is shaped something like a slipper. The body of the paramecium is covered with short cilia which the animal uses to swim about.

If you watch closely enough, you will see that paramecia swim by trial and error. If you put a few grains of dirt in the water, the paramecium will swim along until it bumps into one of the grains. Then it will back up, turn slightly, and swim forward again. If it doesn't turn far enough, and bumps into the obstruction once more, it will again back up, turn a bit more, and try again. It will continue to act this way until it is able to swim past the obstruction. This behavior is called avoidance reaction.

Paramecia are kept alive in almost every school laboratory. You can keep them alive in a small vial of water by feeding them grains of starch, yeast, or small algae.

Paramecia increase by dividing, and in one of the photographs you can see a paramecium that is almost finished turning into two by division.

This division of one organism into two organisms is called binary fission. The nucleus, the dark mass of protoplasm you can see inside the organism, divides first. Then the body of the animalcule itself thins in the middle until it is merely a thread, with one half of the nucleus inside each half of the organism's body. The thread then parts and the creature becomes two creatures, each with a nucleus. A paramecium may divide as many as three times in one day.

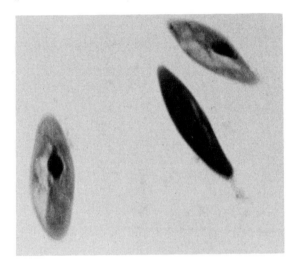

Paramecia.

A paramecium undergoing fission, a method of reproduction.

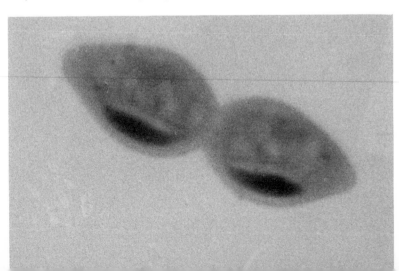

Other protozoa divide many more times than that each day.

The same drop of water in which you found paramecia might contain another protozoan called a didinium. This animal looks like a little round jug with a tiny spout on the top, which is its mouth.

The didinium feeds on paramecia. It swims up to the animal, fastens its mouth against the paramecium, and then opens its mouth so wide that it is able to swallow the paramecium whole! A didinium will eat a great many paramecia, one after the other.

Didiniums, like most protozoa, swim by means of cilia. Each animals has two rings of short cilia around its body, one near the top just under the base of the mouth projection, and the other around the middle.

In the seas and oceans of the world live a group of animals called coelenterates, from the Greek words meaning "cavity" and "intestine." These animals have a muscular tube with a gullet at the top which serves as their digestive tract. Within this group are included anemones, which, when they are opened and looking for food, look like flowers. Related to the anemones, but living in the water of your pond or drainage ditch, is a tiny animal called a hydra.

These didiniums eat all the paramecia they can find.

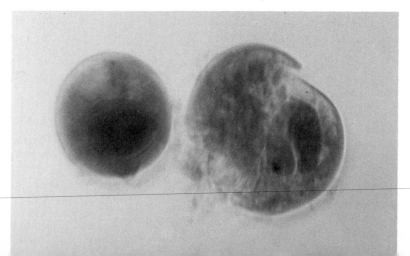

A hydra is a coelenterate, too. It is free swimming, and can also walk with a curious tumbling-head-over-heels motion.

A hydra is composed of a tube within a double wall. Between the two walls is a jellylike substance. The open top of the tube is the mouth. The closed bottom of the tube forms a disc with which the hydra can anchor itself to obtain food.

Around the opening of the top of the hydra are tentacles nearly as long as the oganism's body. The hydra feeds on other protozoa and on small plant life by trapping this food with its long tentacles. The hydra bends the tentacles downward to stuff food into its mouth and then straightens them up again to search for more to eat.

A hydra reproduces by forming a bud on one wall. The bud grows larger and larger until it is big enough and complete enough to break away from the parent hydra.

The photograph clearly shows the double walls, the disc-like floor at the bottom, and the tentacles of the hydra. You can also see two buds just starting to grow into long tubes like the parent animal.

Another animal which is very common and easy to find in a drop of pond water is the planaria. Planaria are also called flatworms, because they are indeed very flat and thin.

Flatworms have several odd characteristics. For one thing the proboscis, or mouth, of the animal is in its middle. In the photograph you can see the long proboscis lying flat, right in the center of the creature.

Another curious fact about flatworms is their remarkable power of regeneration. If the flatworm loses a part of itself, even its head, it can grow a new one quite easily. If you took a live flatworm and with a fine, sharp blade split it in two through the head, right between its eyes, very soon it would grow two complete heads, each with two eyes and all the parts of the first head. If you then split the two new heads the same way, the flatworm would grow four heads. The animal will keep on growing two heads for every one you split!

Another curious animal that you can find in your drop of pond water is the cyclops, a one-eyed organism, named after the mythical Greek giant with one eye. Cyclops make little hopping motions when they swim. On close examination, they resemble shrimp. Cyclops are crustaceans, animals with a hard outer skeleton. This makes them a relative of the shrimp, lobster, and crab, which are also crustaceans.

Some cyclops are transparent, or colorless. Others are green, blue, or pink, and some may even be black or red! Usually the ones living near the surface of the water are colorless, while those living in deeper water are colored.

Cyclops feed on microscopic plant life, and are themselves eaten by larger animals and fishes.

The cyclops in the photograph is a male. Females have two sacks of eggs, one hanging from either side, just at the base, of the body.

In the same pond from which you took your "microzoo," you should be able to find numerous tiny plants. With a large dipper of some kind, dip out some more pond water and pour it into a white plastic or enamel container. Then watch it closely. You may see some tiny green balls floating through the clear water. Carefully catch a couple of these by sucking them up with an eyedropper, and then put them in a small vial of water to carry them home. Put them in a cavity slide to examine them.

These little green balls which seem to roll through the water are colonies of volvox. They look like a plant, be-

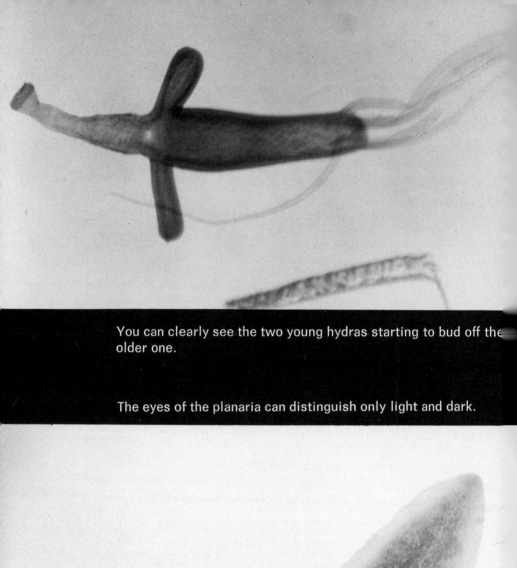

You can clearly see the two young hydras starting to bud off the older one.

The eyes of the planaria can distinguish only light and dark.

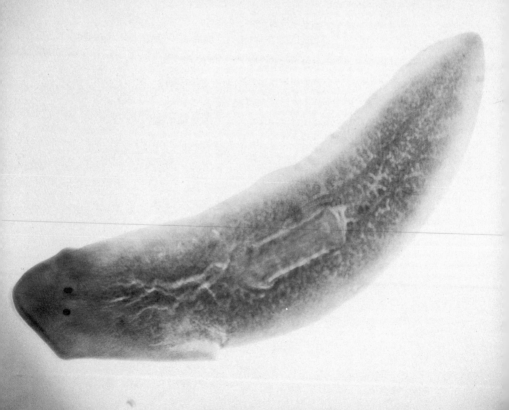

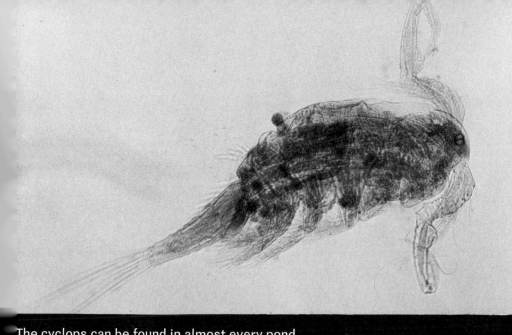

The cyclops can be found in almost every pond.

Most of these volvox colonies show very clearly the "daughter" colonies growing inside them.

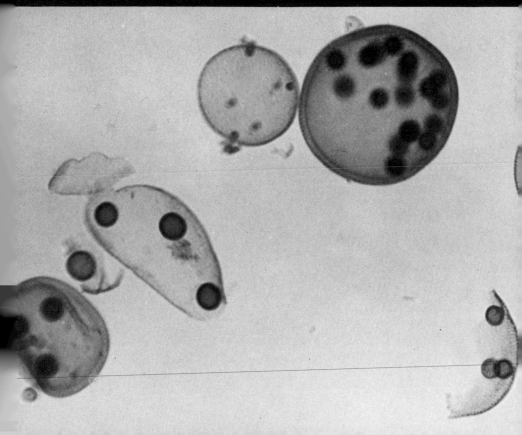

cause they are grass green. Each ball, about 1/10 inch in diameter, consists of gelatinous material in which are embedded thousands of tiny, oval volvox. Each has a long thread, or flagellum, extending from the end. These waving threads, which stick out all over the ball, help the colony of volvox to roll through the water.

Volvox moves through the water with the same side always toward the front. In the rear side of the ball the colony reproduces daughter colonies within itself. In the spring, the ball breaks down and these daughter colonies are released to grow and reproduce in like fashion.

Earlier I mentioned picking a few pieces of algae from the pond water to take home. Now take a look at this material. Pick up a few strands on the point of a fine needle and place them onto a slide. Drop a cover glass over it, letting a small drop of water remain on the algae.

These long threads of green algae are known as spirogyra. Each thread is like a tiny tube, and is composed of many individual cells. Within the cells is dark material running in spiral patterns. This dark material is chlorophyll, which provides food for the spirogyra by converting sunlight into sugar.

When the time comes for spirogyra to reproduce, two strands line themselves up alongside one another. A tiny tube begins to grow from each strand, reaching out to touch the other strand. These tubes touch each other at the tips and grow together. Then the end walls break down, opening the tube to both strands.

The spiral material within one cell starts to flow through the connecting tube into the other cell, where it mingles with the spiral material of the second cell. Up to this point, there is no way of telling which strand is male and which female. The strand which empties *into* the other strand is the male strand, and the one which *receives* the material is the female strand. The material mingles together, then forms an oval mass, called a zygote, within the female cell. This cell falls to the bottom of the pond, becomes buried in the mud, and there passes the winter. In the spring it starts to grow and soon becomes a new strand of spirogyra adding its form and color to the mass from which it grew.

These strands of spirogyra are reproducing through a process called conjugation.

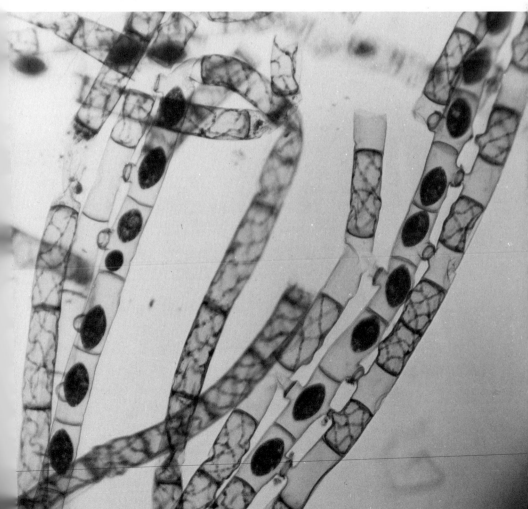

Pick out some twigs or old leaves from the bottom of the pond. Feel them gently. If any feel slippery or slimy, put them into a jar of water to take home. You may have a colony of stentor, a protozoan shaped like a horn, or trumpet. Stentor attaches itself to dead twigs, leaves, and other debris in the pond and lives in colonies of from a few to thousands. They are attached by the small end, and can stretch out many times their normal length in search of food. The large end has an opening which is the mouth. Food is drawn into the mouth by the action of rows of cilia which vibrate rapidly in a circular motion.

A drop of the ooze from the bottom of the pond, diluted with clear water and spread on a slide, should reveal a number of organisms called diatoms. Diatoms are actually shells of microscopic algae, and they come in a great many shapes and sizes. In the photograph, the three which look

Stentors can stretch out several times their length in order to capture food.

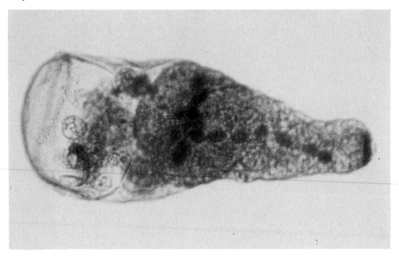

like little barrels, or stacks of deep dishes, are colored red, blue, yellow, and green. They sparkle with an iridescence under the lens.

As small as they are, diatoms occur in such numbers that they form layers many feet thick. In California there are great deposits of diatomaceous earth, which is used for filtering and in polishing and scouring compounds.

Diatoms occur in even greater numbers in salt water. In the seas, one cubic foot of water may contain as many as ten or twelve million diatoms! These diatoms comprise a large proportion of plankton, the mass of minute plants and animals that are the most important link in the food chain in the sea. There are actually two kinds of plankton—phytoplankton, which is all the plant life of the sea, including the diatoms and other algae, and zooplankton, which is the almost microscopic larvae of crustaceans, worms, mollusks, and other animals.

Another very beautiful shell is that of the radiolarian, a protozoan which makes its shell out of calcium and silicon. Countless billions of radiolaria live in the oceans, sometimes as deep as three miles! When alive the animal generally lives near the top of the water until the ocean gets warm from the sun; then it descends for a distance until night, when the water cools again. These animals are a part of the zooplankton I mentioned before.

The best way to examine radiolaria is on a commercial slide which can be purchased for less than a dollar in school-supply houses. Ask for a slide of *Radiolaria strew*. On this slide you will have thousands of specimens and most of them will be differently shaped! Usually the calcium part of the shell is dissolved in the ocean after the animal dies, and the part that remains is silicon.

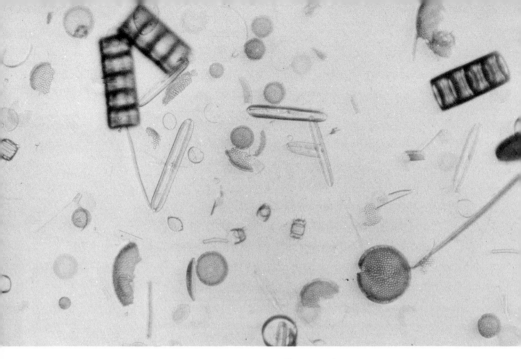

Diatoms come in thousands of different shapes.

The variously shaped radiolaria are among the most beautiful protozoa.

A final suggestion for something you can examine is the life history of the aurelia, a species of jellyfish. If you take a trip to the seashore some warm day in spring, there is a very good possibility that you can find a colony of aurelia hydroids, a stage of the aurelia's life that looks very like a hydra. Otherwise, commercial slides of the various stages of the aurelia may easily be obtained.

The aurelia starts out in life as a planula larva, which looks like a kind of flatworm, without the head or eyes. Planula are free swimming, so the chances of your catching any are very slim.

However, if you examine strands of seaweed, small sticks soaking in the shallow water of the ocean, rocks, or any other debris, you may see a colony of slippery things growing. These may be a colony of the scyphistoma stage of the aurelia. The planula, after hatching from the adult jellyfish, swims around until it finds a good spot, then attaches itself to this spot and becomes the scyphistoma.

The scyphistoma grows until it develops into the next stage, which is called the strobilus. Your colony will probably contain some aurelia at the strobilus stages, too. As the strobilus grows, it develops into a stack of flat creatures, which looks very like a stack of tiny saucers. As the strobilus matures, the "saucers" start breaking away from the top, one at a time. These organisms are free swimming, and are called ephyra.

If you examine the ephyra photograph, you will see that it is divided into eight parts. The four structures in the center of the ephyra will develop into the sex glands of the adult jellyfish. As the ephyra grows, it slowly fills out the spaces between each eighth part, until it finally develops into the mature jellyfish, called the medusa.

In the medusa stage you can recognize the jellyfish. The medusa grows until it reaches the maximum size of that particular species. In the case of aurelia, this is four or five inches in diameter. A medusa looks like a half of a balloon with a fringe around the edge and a tube hanging down from the four center parts. It swims around with the flat, hollow side of its body facing down. Sometimes aurelia are so plentiful that the water near shore is thick with their numbers!

An aurelia planula larva, the first stage in the life of a jellyfish.

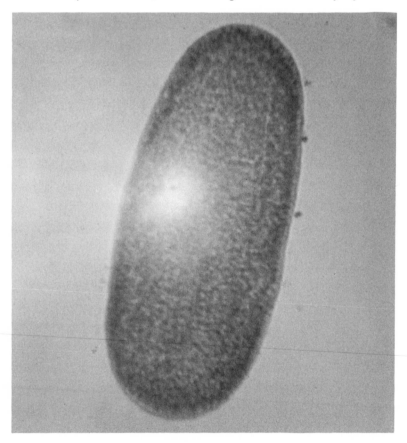

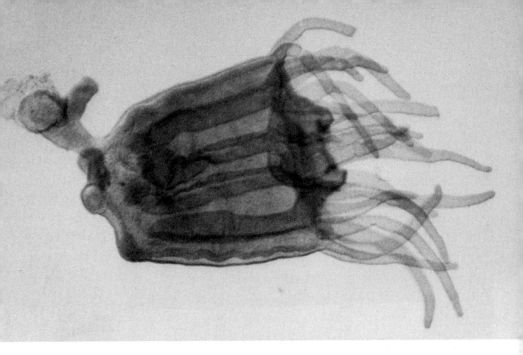

The aurelia scyphistoma is the second stage in a jellyfish's development.

The strobilus stage of the aurelia is the last of the hydroid stages.

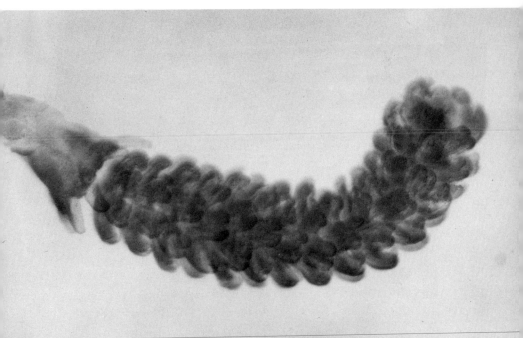

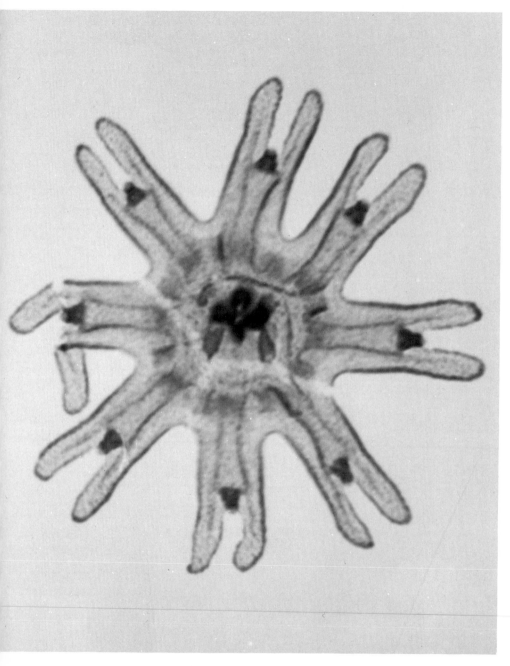

In the ephyra stage, the aurelia is beginning to look something like a jellyfish.

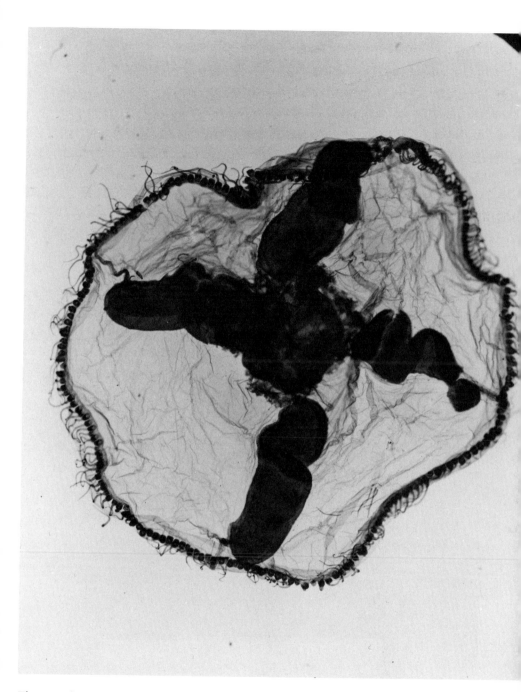

The aurelia medusa is the final stage. Now the jellyfish will grow
to its full size and begin the cycle all over again.

5

Water and Air Pollution

SINCE MOST POLLUTION OF WATER AND OF SOIL IS CHEMICAL rather than biological, the microscope is of little use in detecting the pollutants. Chemical tests readily reveal the matter, but they are not within the scope of this volume. In air, however, and in water, there occur bacteria or protozoa which are a mark of pollution, and these can be seen with the microscope.

There is an excellent experiment which you can perform using *Euglena gracilis*, an algae you can find in almost any pond. Or you can get a culture of this algae from laboratory-supply companies.

Almost any pond will have some euglena in it, and you can easily identify this algae by its shape and its movement. Although it appears to be round, a euglena's shape is roughly triangular, with a small notch on the wide end, which is the front. From this notch grows a long, slender flagellum, or threadlike whip. This flagellum is so fine that it is almost indistinguishable, and under the low-power microscopes you are using, it will rarely, if ever, be seen. However, the rapid, circular movement of the flagellum can be detected under the proper illumination by the movement of the particles in the water.

In motion, a euglena alternately pushes its body out in front, then squeezes it up like an accordion, drawing the rear part forward as it does so. The movement of the euglena is so distinctive that the term *euglenoid movement* is used to describe the similar motion of other organisms with flagella.

To conduct this experiment, set up a small aquarium, about ten gallons or larger, in a location where it will get some direct sunlight each day. The more sunlight it receives, the more rapidly our experiment will progress. You may fill the aquarium with only water, or you may include some clean gravel in the bottom and a few aquarium plants. A couple of fish—either guppies or zebra fish are the least expensive—may also be a good addition to the tank. Leave the tank uncovered, or leave at least a small opening on top.

Place some euglena in the tank. This may be either wild material you have gathered from a pond, or a culture purchased for a small sum from a school-biological-supply company.

Now watch the water, and in a few days you will see the euglena beginning to multiply more and more rapidly, until the water begins to turn green. Of course, you must feed the fish in the tank, as you would if you were keeping tropical fish in a regular aquarium. Do not overfeed the fish, however; a tiny pinch of fish food daily is all that is needed.

As the water gets greener, you will note that the fish begin to come to the top of the water more frequently, gulping air as they break the surface. Finally the water will become "pea soup," so green you can hardly see through it. Now smell the water each day, and you will find that it will begin to smell bad after a time. The fish may survive a few days longer; but as the water increases its stink, they will finally die. Remove the fish, but do not otherwise disturb the tank. The water will become more and more foul smelling, until finally it will begin to lessen in smell. Still leave it alone, and the foul, polluted water will finally stop smelling entirely.

Now an amazing process begins. Slowly the water will clear itself, until finally it is once more more clean and sparkling—so crystal clear that the tank appears empty. What has happened is this. When first put into the tank, the water contained the usual amount of dissolved minerals and oxygen. Then you put in the euglena, and the algae began to multiply. The euglena utilized minerals and oxygen from the water; and, as they multiplied more and more, the supply of minerals and oxygen slowly became less and less, since you were not replenishing them as they were consumed.

In time the numbers of euglena reached such proportions that the water first turned green, then became like pea soup. Now there was not enough food to support these countless millions of algae, so they began to die from lack of both food (minerals) and oxygen. As they died, the water began to smell bad. The water in the tank was now polluted. As the pollution progressed, there remained insufficient oxygen to support the fish, so they, too, died. No normal life could now live in the water. In fact, the only things that could survive were creatures called anaerobic bacteria, bacteria which can live without oxygen. The anaerobic bacteria began to consume the dead euglena, decomposing the algae and utilizing them as food. This gradual decomposition removed further oxygen from the water.

The decomposition of the algae continues until the tank is really foul smelling. Then, as the anaerobic bacteria continue to consume and break down the algae, their food, in turn, becomes less and less plentiful, so they begin to die as well. As they die the water begins to clear, until, finally, when all the anaerobic bacteria are gone, the water is once more clean and clear.

Now you may continue the experiment. You have some water which was polluted, and is now clear. Without disturbing the tank or agitating the water, drop in another small fish. It should not survive very long, since the water has been depleted of all its minerals and all its oxygen.

Now take a gallon or so of the water and, placing it in a clean jug, shake it vigorously for a time, to aerate it. Pour it back into the tank, then repeat this operation two or three times more, taking a gallon of the water from the tank, shaking it, and replacing it. Now drop in a fish and see what happens. It should show no distress.

In your own home you have just performed nearly the identical cycle that the major water sources throughout the world are undergoing. Take as an example Lake Erie. This lake is polluted to the point where practically nothing at all can live in the water. The pollution was caused by an excess of phosphate materials being dumped into the lake

over many, many years. Finally the phosphates reached a
level that permitted algae to take over and to grow so rapidly that they consumed the minerals just as they did in
your tank. The water then was taken over by the anaerobic
bacteria, and the lake became foul and polluted. This is
what has been happening around the world, until the pollution of water sources has become a critical affair.

With a high-powered microscope it is possible to examine many of the different particles floating in the air, although you may not be able to identify them. (As you have
seen, pollen is different. Even a fairly low-powered microscope will reveal the shape of pollen grains of the ragweed,
for example.)

An excellent way to examine the pollution of the air is to
use a ruled microscope slide obtainable from school-laboratory-supply companies. A plain slide may also be used, and
you may put on the rulings with a grease pencil (a glass-
marking crayon) or by laying a small piece of plain window
screening over the slide while examining it in your microscope.

To prepare the slide for these air pollution tests, place a
small blob of petroleum jelly on one surface about an inch
from one end. With the end of a second slide, smear this
grease across the slide to within an inch of the opposite end.
The grease smear should be even and very thin, with just
enough grease left on the glass to make the surface sticky. A
little practice will enable you to smear a slide in one quick
motion, lifting the surplus grease up off the slide with the
spreader. The ends should be left clean and dry simply
because you need an area to handle the slide with, and
because the center is the only portion you will have under
examination.

You might prepare several such slides, then store them in a slide box away from dust, light, and heat until they are needed.

You may use these slides in several different ways. (First of all, you should keep a record of what you are doing; otherwise the results will be meaningless to you or to anyone else.) If you are marking the slide with a glass-marking pencil or grease pencil, the glass should be ruled *before* the grease is smeared. The ruling is applied to one side of the slide and the grease smeared on the opposite side. The rulings should be evenly spaced, and not more than a millimeter apart. They should be put on in both directions, to make a series of squares all over the center portion of the slides.

An alternate way to obtain this ruling is to use a square of fly screening once the slide is placed under the microscope. Carefully lay this screen on top of the greased side, and hold it in position with a piece of adhesive tape of any kind. If the tape is wrapped around the slide at the two ends, the center portion will be left clear for your use.

Now the prepared slide should be exposed to the air for a given period of time, and at an established time of the day (or night). A suggested schedule would be at 8:00 A.M., noon, and 6:00 P.M. A good exposure period would be two hours. At 8:00 A.M. lay a slide greasy face up in an open location for two hours; then bring it indoors and place it in a covered box, such as a slide box. Be sure you label it with the length and time of exposure. At noon of the same day expose a second slide for two hours, placing the slide *in the same location as before*. This slide also should be placed in a protective box after the two-hour exposure. The third slide is exposed for the same length of time, in the same location, at six o'clock at night of the same day.

Now you have a series of slides from which you may make your determination of the pollution on that particular day. Be sure to make a record of the kind of day it was—clear, still, windy, and so on. As a matter of fact, you should make several series of the exposures on different kinds of days: a clear, still day; a clear, windy day; immediately after a rainstorm; during a rainstorm; and under any other weather conditions that you might experience. The series may be carried further, into the different seasons—experimenting with the same weather conditions in summer, winter, spring, and fall.

After the slides have been exposed to the air, take a particle count through your microscope. A 100-power microscope should be the lowest you use. Higher power can be used, but you need not go over 250 power. Determine first the number of squares you are going to use for your count, and never vary this number. Say, for example, that you are going to count ten squares on each slide. Count the particles adhering to the greased surface within one square as accurately as you possibly can; then mark the number down on a pad. Rest your eye a moment, then count the next square, marking that number down as well. Continue this way until you have counted all the particles in the entire ten squares; then add up the total. These ten squares you have counted will be your pollution index.

By counting the same number of squares on each slide, you may make a rather accurate comparison of the air pollution at different times of the day, on different kinds of days, and at different times of the year. Specific information like this is taken all over the country by weather stations and pollution-watch crews, and the records are so accurate and reliable that they are often used in courts as evidence.

A person being tried for some offense can claim he was unable to see well because of the overcast or dusty air, but the records might show that at that time on that day the air had only a couple thousand particles per cubic centimeter, making it very clear. All kinds of conditions can be substantiated by this simple but classic type of air pollution test.

After a few such tests have been made, you will be able to begin to identify certain kinds of pollutants on your slides. Throughout the year, pollen grains will be the most common, and, as I stated earlier, these are so distinctive that the plant they come from may be identified by its pollen grains. In the spring and early summer, pollen from trees will be more common than other kinds. As the summer progresses, flower pollen will supplant that from the trees. In the fall, daisies, ragweed, goldenrod, and similar plants send their pollen into the air for reproduction.

If you make a series of permanent slides of various pollens taken directly from the plants and flowers as they ripen, labeling each slide accurately with the name of the plant and the time of the year the pollen was taken, you will be able to use this file to identify the air pollution at any time of the year.

It will be interesting, also, to try to identify the other particles found on your test slides. If you live near a manufacturing district, the slides should show particles thrown from industrial smokestacks. Cement factories are among the biggest air polluters, and the sharp, abrasive grains of cement are surely to be seen if you live within even miles of such a plant.

7

Photographing Your Microscopic Specimens

MANY READERS MAY WANT TO TRY THEIR HAND AT TAKING photographs of the things they see through the microscope, so I will tell you a little of how to go about this fascinating hobby.

First of all, you need a camera of the single-lens reflex type. These are now the most popular kind of camera on the market, and there are literally dozens of different brands and prices available. The camera should have inter-changeable lenses, and should focus through the lens.

Next you need, of course, a microscope which gives a good image, and one which has provision for attaching a camera to it. This attachment may be in the form of a short tube that you can slip into the top of the microscope in place of the ocular, or it may be in the form of a special microscope attachment supplied by different camera manufacturers to fit their specific cameras. This you will have to determine by the kind of camera you buy. Whatever type of camera and attaching tube you use, the object is to adjust the camera *without its lens* to the tube of the microscope.

Even if the microscope you have does not have a removable ocular—the little Bausch and Lomb school microscopes do not—with a little ingenuity you might be able to make a tube to slip over the tube of the microscope and hold your camera. Even a tube of stiff cardboard may be adjustable to the instrument, with the camera held to it with masking tape or adhesive tape.

You *must* be sure that the image thrown into the air within the microscope is able to be focused on the film plane of the camera. This usually cannot be done with the lens on the camera, which is the reason an interchangeable-lens camera is needed. The reason the camera lens cannot focus the image from the microscope is that a camera lens is made to focus images at distances of from several feet to many hundreds of feet. The image in the microscope tube is merely a few inches from the camera's focal plane. If you used the lens on the camera, the tube attaching it to the microscope would have to be several feet long, the minimal focusing distance of the camera lens, making the operation most impractical.

You also need a source of good, strong light in order to expose your film. Microscope lights are available and are the easiest to use. When you are photographing prepared microscope slides of specimens, the light can be softer, since the inanimate slide will not move during the exposure and you can take what amounts to time exposures to get the proper negative. If, however, you are working with living material, the exposure must be very short—from 1/250 to 1/1000 of a second—and you must have enough light to expose the film properly.

This amount of light brings up another problem—that of heat. An intense light sent through the microscope will heat up the slide, and you will find that in a very short time the water containing your specimens is so hot that the animals have all been killed. The water may even evaporate while you are working to get a good image and focus.

The use of very high-speed film such as Tri X Pan or Ansco Super Hypan may help, but this film is very grainy in the emulsion, and cameras such as we have to use with the microscope are only 35 mm film size. By the time we get an enlargement of the tiny film, the grain is so bad that all detail in the photograph is lost. A compromise can be made by using a medium-speed film, like Plus X or Versapan, which will help a little, but it is still best to use the finest-grain film available, Panatomic-X or Isopan FF, which, by its very nature, is slow-speed exposure.

There is now a developing system available which will enable you to use a slow-speed emulsion at higher speeds and still get a perfectly exposed negative. This developer is called Acufine, and it is available in almost every camera store. A list of adjusted speeds is available from the dealer which will tell you the speed you can use to expose your particular film when developing it in Acufine. Acufine greatly increases the practical speed of the emulsion of your film, and still leaves it as fine grained as the film would be when exposed at its normal speed. Usually, extending the developing time beyond the normal limit kills the fine-grain properties of a film, but this is not the case with Acufine. (An even finer-grain developer is Diafine, made by the same company, but this becomes a bit cumbersome when used by an amateur in the home.)

In the event your dealer does not have any of the exposure lists when you buy your developer, I list here for your convenience some of the adjusted speeds:

Film (35mm)	Acufine exposure index	Development time in minutes		
		65'	70'	75'
Kodak Tri-X	1200	6	4¾	3¼
Kodak Plus-X	320	5	4	3¼
Kodak Panatomic-X	100	2½	2	1¾
Agfa Isopan FF	64	2½	2	1¾
Adox KB-14	64	2½	2	1¾
Ansco Super Hypan	1000	8¾	7	5½
Ansco Versapan	250	4¾	3¾	3

Of the above emulsions, the Panatomic-X and the Isopan FF are the finest grained. I use nothing but Panatomic-X myself, and have used this film since it was put on the market many, many years ago. If you use Acufine, be sure that whatever emulsion you use you follow the listing for exposure factors and development times as given above or on the sheet from your dealer.

Films are rated in this country according to a factor called ASA Speed. This is a guide from which you may calculate the proper exposure for a given photograph. Most exposure meters are based on this ASA factor, and you read the exposure directly off the scale. However, exposure meters are difficult to use when taking photographs through a microscope, and are inaccurate at best.

If you are fortunate enough to possess a camera with an exposure meter built in to work through the lens, you may get an accurate exposure reading through its use. Otherwise you must take test shots, developing them as you go along to determine what the best exposure time is.

As a guide, I suggest using either of the fine-grain, slow-speed films (Panatomic-X or Isopan FF) to take exposures of one-half second, one second, and three seconds as a first test. Develop this film and look at the negatives when they are dry. You should be able to tell whether any of these exposures were good, and, if none are satisfactory, what exposure to try next. Always bracket your exposures one speed below and one speed above the speed you think is the best. The film emulsion will have enough latitude to produce a usable negative with a slight over- or underexposure.

You may develop your films at home, even if you do not have a photographic darkroom, by using any one of the many kinds of daylight developing tanks sold in camera stores. You may shut yourself inside a closet, placing a heavy towel or other material on the floor along the inside of the door to exclude light. If light leaks around the edges of the door, additional cloths may be hung with thumbtacks to cover the area.

As a matter of fact, light of which you may be unaware may still ruin the film if it strikes it. The best thing to do before using any particular closet is to get inside, fix the cloths in place, stand with your eyes shut for several minutes, and then open them and see if you can spot any stray light. (Holding your eyes closed for a time will open the irises, permitting you to see weak light easily.) The lights in the room outside the closet should be turned out and all window shades drawn down before you enter the closet to load the film.

Always turn your back to the door when loading the film in the tank. Shield the film by holding it in front of your body, working with your arms clamped to your sides, just in case there is any stray light.

After the film is in the tank, you may take it out into the lighted room to process it. The developer and the fixer should be mixed and ready in bottles. You should also have a source of water handy. It is perfectly all right to do the work at the kitchen sink or the bathroom basin, since neither the developer nor the fixer are poured down the drain. Both are returned to their bottles after use, to be used again and again as you take more photographs.

Develop the film for the indicated time, and then, using a funnel in the mouth of the bottle, pour the developer out of the tank and back into its proper bottle. Rinse the funnel. Immediately fill the tank with water from the faucet, until the tank overflows. Now pour the water out down the drain and immediately pour fixer into the tank. Fix for the proper time. Then, using the rinsed funnel, pour the fixer into its own bottle.

Now wash the film in running water for not less than fifteen minutes, and then hang it up to dry. Wooden or plastic spring-clothespins are good for hanging film. There are also plastic pins with a hook on the end which makes it convenient to hang the film on the shower rod or on a line. A second clip should be fastened to the bottom end of the film strip to stretch it out as it dries.

For making the paper prints, you do need a darkroom, an enlarger, and some other equipment, so, at least until you become really involved with photography, it might be best—at least it will be easier—to take your negatives to a local store for printing. It goes without saying that you should always handle your negatives by their edges—*never* put your fingers on either the emulsion side or the reverse side of a negative. The fingerprint you leave may very well ruin the negative completely, and if it does, you may depend on it that the negative will be the best one you have ever taken.

Photographing living material through the microscope is very difficult unless you have the special equipment needed for such work. True, with the help of a powerful light you may be able to take pictures of larger protozoa held in a cavity slide. However, you must use a weak light to focus with, turning on the powerful light only for the very short exposure time, then turning it off again, in order to avoid boiling your subjects.

Always use the lowest-power-objective lens you can on the microscope when photographing living material, since the lower the power of the lens, the more light it passes through to the camera. High-powered objectives cut down the light greatly, and may make it impossible for you to get a good exposure within the short time permitted when using a hot, strong light.

The equipment used for taking photographs of living material is complicated and costly. The simplest outfit available, a microprojector with a camera attachment, costs several hundred dollars. And even with this equipment you are up against the difficulty of heat from the light cooking the specimens if they are left in the glare for more than a minute or two. The advantage of this outfit is that you can expose at very high shutter speeds, thereby eliminating the problem of the jerky, erratic motion of the living creatures under high magnification. Some photomicroscopes cost more than $8000, and the attachments available for them may run the cost up to as high as $10,000. Naturally, these are laboratory items for use by research companies, and are not within the reach of the amateur.

Index